# EMBROIDERY KIT

10 Magical Projects inspired by the Wizarding World

**Thunder Bay Press**
An imprint of Printers Row Publishing Group
9717 Pacific Heights Blvd, San Diego, CA 92121
www.thunderbaybooks.com • mail@thunderbaybooks.com

Copyright © 2020 Warner Bros. Entertainment Inc.
WIZARDING WORLD characters, names, and related indicia are
© & ™ Warner Bros. Entertainment Inc.
WB SHIELD: © & ™ WBEI.
Publishing Rights © JKR. (s20)

Printers Row Publishing Group is a division of Readerlink Distribution Services, LLC.
Thunder Bay Press is a registered trademark of Readerlink Distribution Services, LLC.

Correspondence regarding the content of this book should be sent to Thunder Bay Press, Editorial Department, at the above address. Author and illustration inquiries should be sent to BlueRed Press Ltd, 31 Follaton, Plymouth Road, Totnes, Devon, TQ9 5ND.

**Thunder Bay Press**
Publisher: Peter Norton • Associate Publisher: Ana Parker
Senior Developmental Editor: April Graham Farr
Developmental Editor: Diane Cain
Editor: Jessica Matteson
Product Manager: Kathryn C. Dalby
Production Team: Jonathan Lopes, Rusty von Dyl

Produced by BlueRed Press Ltd.
Designed by Insight Design Concepts Ltd.

Author: Deborah Wilding

ISBN: 978-1-68412-891-4

Manufactured, printed, and assembled in Heshan, China

25 24 23 22 21   2 3 4 5 6

DEBORAH WILDING

# EMBROIDERY KIT
10 Magical Projects Inspired by the Wizarding World

# CONTENTS

## KEY TO DIFFICULTY LEVEL

Beginner ................ ⚡

Beginner/Intermediate...... ⚡⚡

Intermediate .............. ⚡⚡⚡

Advanced ................ ⚡⚡⚡⚡

# INTRODUCTION

Welcome! These embroidery designs have been inspired by the magical Harry Potter movies and include iconic images and characters closely associated with the Wizarding World.

Embroidery is a simple art form that has been popular for hundreds of years. It can be worked by anyone using the minimum of tools and will create a piece of art that is not only unique to you, but something you can be really proud of. All that's needed is thread, a needle, and fabric—we provide the inspiration!

These projects have been designed to motivate you by creating the Harry Potter characters and motifs you love, but also to teach you a good variety of stitches. This knowledge will help you use your new skills on other embroidery designs in the future.

# Getting Started

## KIT COMPONENTS

For these two projects—"Glasses, Scarves, and Scar" and "Hogwarts Castle"—all the materials are included in our kit box. For all the other projects a list of suggested materials is supplied with the project instructions. Colors can be altered to suit your taste.

# EQUIPMENT

## FABRIC

Hand embroidery is best done on light or medium-weight fabrics like cotton cloth. Thick materials make the stitching very difficult to keep even and neat. In most projects I like to use a backing fabric of calico. This helps stabilize the work, and prevents strong thread colors being seen through the fabric.

## THREADS

Stranded DMC cotton embroidery thread is used for all these projects, and their product numbers have been supplied so you know exactly what to buy to recreate the designs. Additionally, the number of individual threads used at each stage is detailed in the project instructions so you know exactly how many you need to use.

When embroidery thread is supplied in the skein, it comes as a group of six threads. In most cases these threads are divided into the suitable number for the section of the design you are working on. It's always a good idea to split the threads into the individual strands and group them into the correct number needed. When a skein is new, the threads tend to be bunched up and wrapped around each other. By straightening them out you will encounter fewer problems when you are in the middle of stitching.

## NEEDLES

Embroidery needles tend to have a sharp point and a slightly larger and longer eye than a general-purpose sewing needle. Needles for your first two projects are supplied, but it's your preference which size of needle you feel comfortable with. I stitch all the time, so threading needles is not a problem. I like the smallest gauge needle I can use for the thread. When using two strands of DMC try an embroidery needle size 8. For a thicker thread, or more strands of DMC, I like a chenille needle size 22. My advice is to select a needle you can thread easily: it's no fun spending all your precious sewing time fighting with threading the needle.

## SCISSORS

Small sharp-pointed scissors are an essential piece of kit. Try only ever to use your embroidery scissors for threads and fabric— as soon as they are used for paper or card they will blunt and lose some of their sharpness.

## HOOPS AND FRAMES

A 6in (15.5cm) ring frame has been supplied with your kit. This is ideal for supporting and firmly stretching your embroidery fabric. It can also be used to display your work when it's finished. The frame comes apart into two rings, inner and outer. Use the screw fixing to slightly loosen the outer

ring, then the inner ring can slip out. To fit a piece of fabric, put the smaller ring on a flat surface, then place your piece of fabric over the ring so the printed design sits centrally inside the circle of the frame. Place the outer ring over the top and push it down into position, thus pulling the fabric tight. Even out any creases. Once you are happy that the design is in the correct position, you can tighten the screw fixing to ensure the fabric stays put while you are sewing your embroidery.

## OTHER USEFUL ITEMS

Over time you will collect other sewing-related equipment, none of which is essential, but can prove useful from time to time. Items I like to keep to hand include:

- cardboard bobbins—I use these to store and organize my threads in a bobbin box
- pencil and paper
- pins, pin cushion, thimble
- screwdriver—it's an ever-growing sewing kit
- strong heavyweight sewing thread
- watercolors and fabric paints —used to add additional texture and color to the background fabric.

While embroidering I like to use a supporting frame held on a stand. There are lots of different kinds on the market to choose from. I find being able to sew with both hands not only makes the process quicker, but also helps with the accuracy and consistency of my stitching.

## KNOTS

There are many methods for knotting your thread. Whichever method you use, make sure your knot is small and firm, so that the first stitches of embroidery are secure. If you find following the pictures difficult, there are loads of video tutorials available online for all sorts of different methods.

Create a loop by arranging the thread as shown in the photo. [1]

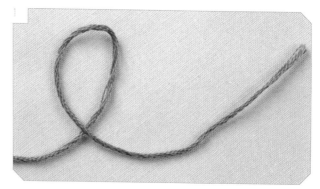

Move the free end of the thread beneath the loop. Using a needle or your finger, bring this thread under the loop and up through the loop. [2]

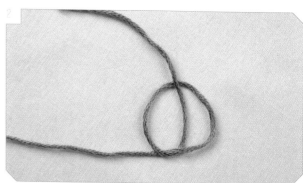

Pull the thread either side of the loop and tighten your knot. [3]

## THREADING A NEEDLE

This can be a little tricky, but with practice becomes easy.
- Trim the threads using sharp scissors so that they are the same length at the end you are threading though the eye of the needle.
- Pinch the thread ends together between your first finger and thumb so only the tips of the threads can be seen.
- Push the eye of the needle over the (still being firmly held) threads.

## STARTING OFF AND ENDING STITCHES

- You can start your stitching with a knot at the back of the fabric. Just try to make sure it is small enough to hold the stitches, but not so big as to cause a bump.
- When you are finished with a color, or the thread being used is becoming too short or damaged, take the thread through to the back of your work and weave in the end 1in (2.5cm) or so into your previous stitching in such a way that the thread is held securely in position. Trim off the excess.

## USING TRANSFERS

This embroidery kit includes iron-on transfers for ten Harry Potter projects, a 6in (15cm) hoop, and two needles, plus the fabric for two projects. To get started you need to iron-on the transfer for your first project.

You need to find a flat, heatproof surface, and a dry iron. Select your project transfer and gently press it, ink side down, onto the center of your fabric.

Gently but firmly, press and iron the transfer using a warm iron. Do not move the transfer during this process. This should only take a few seconds.

Once the design has been transferred to the fabric [1] you are ready to start your stitching.

## USING THE HOOP

Take the wooden hoop and remove the outer hoop from the inner hoop by loosening the screw fixing. [1]

Put the smallest hoop onto a flat clean surface.

Place the calico fabric over the hoop, then place the fabric with the design over the calico. Make certain that the design lies centrally in the middle of your hoop. [2, 3]

Now carefully push the larger embroidery hoop over the fabrics and onto the smaller hoop—this will result in the fabrics being pulled taut between the two hoops. Tighten the screw and make sure there are no creases in the fabrics. [4, 5, 6]

*Note*

Pull the fabric gently all the way round the outside of the frame so it is held firmly in the ring. The tighter the tension, the easier you will find stitching. Also, the more consistent and even the tension is on the fabric, the neater and even your embroidery will be.

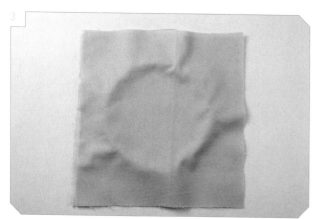

## FINISHING OFF PROJECTS

Stretch the finished design in the hoop: make sure there are no creases. Then trim excess fabric to 1.5in (4cm) around the outside edge of the hoop. [1, 2]

Using a running stitch and strong thread, stitch around excess fabric about 0.75in (2cm) away from edge. [3]

Gently pull on the thread to pull it tight. Knot the ends of the thread together. [4]

I like also to lace the back of the work so the finished embroidery stays nice and flat. To do this, use a long, light but strong, thread stitch across the back, working round in a circle and pulling the thread firmly. [5]

To finish off the design, cover the back with fabric. First cut out a circle in card just slightly small than the hoop—you can mark this out in advance by drawing round the inner edge of your smallest embroidery wooden hoop.

Cut out a suitable backing fabric slightly larger than the card. Using a running stitch, stitch round the edge of the fabric and pull the threads tight when finished. [6, 7]

When the backing card is covered, slip stitch the backing onto the hoop. Position the covered card in the middle leaving an equal gap round all the edges. Slide the threaded needle along the edge of the covered card and then through the back of the fabric on the reverse of your embroidery. Make all these stitches about 0.25in (5mm) long. Work around the whole circle and finish off the thread neatly when complete. [8]

Stretch the finished design.

4

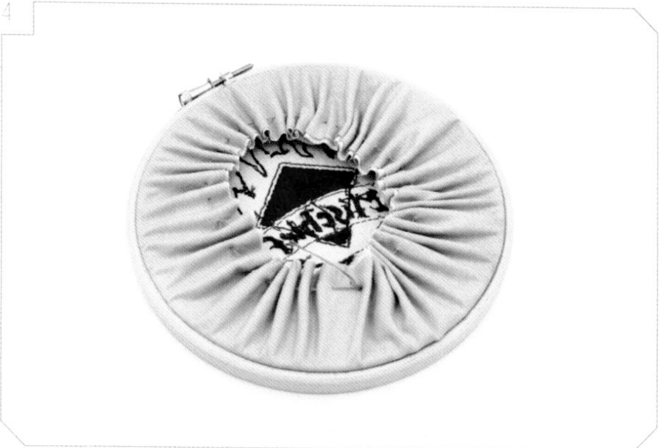

7

5

8

6

BEWARE moving STAIRCASES
BEWARE Boggart IN THIS CLOSET!
to HOGSMEADE
LOWER Chambers corridor North-East
Porticus Imago
LOWER Chambers Portrait CORRIDOR
ROOM of DOOM
PROWLING passage
The Dark FOREST

Stitches

The embroideries are made up of basic stitches used in lots of different styles to create many different finishes and effects. The same shapes can be put together using stitches with different methods and colors—all of which makes the finished item look really different. The only things that vary are the size of the stitches used, the threads used, the colors, and the base fabric.

Using our pre-planned, detailed, designs will help you build your stitching and color confidence. Whether you chose to just outline a shape, or totally fill that shape with stitching, will really change the overall effect. It's up to you!

## BACK STITCH

This is a line of equal length stitches.

From the back, bring the needle up through the fabric and gently pull a straight stitch along the line you are following. Push the needle back through the fabric, bringing the needle up through the fabric ready to create the next stitch. Make a surface stitch filling the gap by taking the needle through the fabric in the shared hole of the previous stitch (rather than moving forward along the line).

Moving forward, bring the needle up on the line, leaving enough space to create the new back stitch. This sequence continues along the length of the line to be covered.

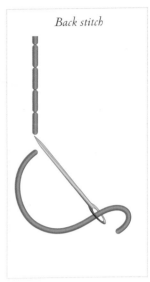

*Back stitch*

*Chain stitch*

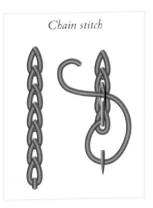

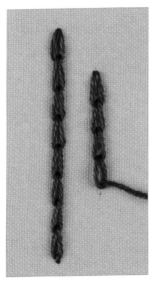

*Detached chain stitch*

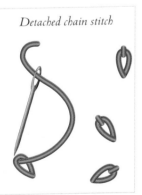

## CHAIN STITCH/DETACHED CHAIN STITCH

Chain stitch produces a line of even-sized stitches. From the back, bring the needle up at the start of the line to be covered. Take the needle and thread it back through the same hole to create a loop the size you want. Holding onto the loop, bring the needle back through the fabric at the end of the loop, and pass it through that loop to create the next unit of chain stitch. Allow the loop to tighten around the new thread, pulling in the direction you are traveling. Take the needle back into the same hole inside the chain stitch loop to create a new loop, and repeat. When your line is complete, make a final stitch as a securing stitch at the end. This small stitch is taken through the fabric to the outside of a loop so that the last loop in the sequence is held firm and the line cannot be pulled out.

Detached chain stitches (aka lazy daisy stitches) are separate chain-stitch units. Bring the needle up through the fabric in the position required, take the needle down in the same hole holding onto the loop. Bring the needle back through the fabric inside the loop and tighten the thread. Secure the loop in position with a small holding stitch at the base.

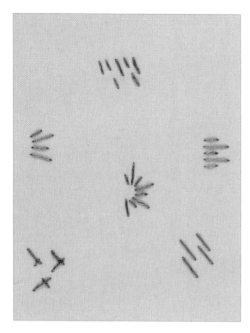

*Decorative straight stitch*

## DECORATIVE STRAIGHT STITCH

Used to create fine detail at any time, straight stitches can be sewn on the surface of the fabric—they are used when the line is not too long.

Overlong straight stitches are often held down to prevent them looking loose or catching on things. If the stitches are fine and not overly long, just straight stitches will work.

## TASSELS

These decorative flourishes can really embellish a piece of needlework. Cut a bunch of threads twice the length you want your finished tassel to be. Bring a threaded needle up through the fabric at the position you want to attach the tassel.

Stitch over the threads, while holding them tightly. Once the bunch is held firmly, bring all the threads together. Now, working across the entire bunched threads, secure them together by stitching over the bunch a couple of times to create the neck of the tassel.

Once the tassel is in place and secured to the fabric, the loose ends can be trimmed to even them up.

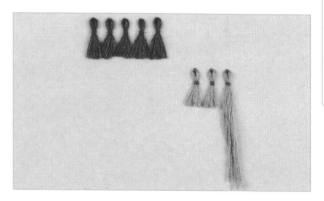

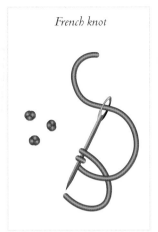

*French knot*

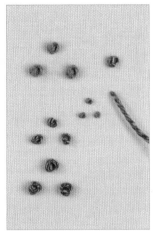

## FRENCH KNOTS

From behind, bring the needle out of the fabric where you want to create the French knot, holding the thread out to the left under tension (to the right if you are left-handed). While holding the needle in your right hand and working from above, wrap the thread (as many times as you want) around the needle, all the time keeping it under tension. Place the tip of the needle into the fabric and slide the thread wrap down the needle until it comes into contact with the fabric. The needle is then taken through the fabric and the excess thread pulled through to the back of the fabric leaving the knot in place. Leave a small space between where the thread came up and where the needle goes through the fabric so the knot has a tiny bit of fabric to sit on, otherwise it will wobble and be insecure.

## RUNNING STITCH

Small stitches created in a line, the stitches themselves are equal in length with the gap between them consistent in size. Bring the needle up through the fabric and create a straight stitch on the line you are following. Take the needle back through the fabric and repeat the process keeping the stitches and the gaps between the stitches even.

Running stitch can be made with gaps but you can also fill the gaps with a variation called double running stitch. When you have completed your line in running stitch, go back over the same line, this time creating a stitch on the surface where you had gaps. You will end up with a solid line of stitches.

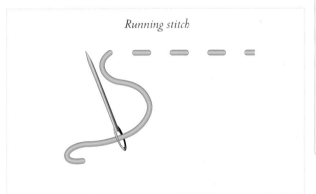

*Running stitch*

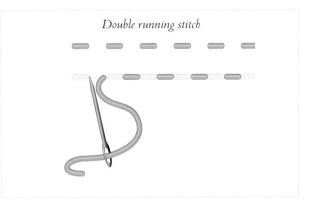

*Double running stitch*

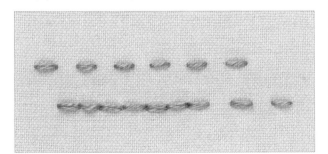

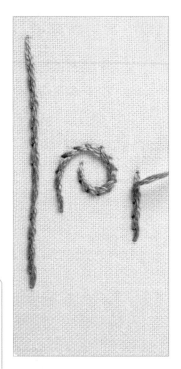

*Stem stitch*

## STEM STITCH

This stitch creates a delicate twisted rope effect to the line. This is achieved by making sure stitches start beneath straight stitches and "push" them to one side.

Start with bringing the needle up through the fabric at the beginning of the line. Take the needle down on the line, but rather than pulling the thread all the way through the fabric, hold a loop of thread on the surface of the fabric. Holding the loop to the right-hand side of the line, bring the needle through the fabric at the midpoint between these two stitches. Once the thread is pulled through you will have a stitch over the line with the new thread piece coming out beneath the stitch. Create the next stitch at an equal length to the first. Again, hold the loop you create to the right and bring the needle up in the same hole as the last stitch ended. Pull the thread through and repeat.

### Note

Stitches should be of equal length, but when you are going round tight curves, the stitches will need to be a little shorter so you can accurately follow the curves.

## SPLIT STITCH

A small stitch created in a line, the stitches themselves are equal in length. Bring the needle up through the fabric and create a straight stitch on the line you are following, bring the needle back up through the stitch you created, thus splitting the stitch in half. The same method is repeated along the line.

Split stitch creates an accurate firm line which is used both as a decorative stitch and a structural stitch when you are outlining areas which will be filled with satin stitch or long and short stitch.

*Split stitch*

## LONG AND SHORT

Shapes can be filled in and shaded in color with a technique called long and short. This method of embroidery uses either two strands together or a single strand of embroidery thread. In the example photos, single strands of three shades of brown have been used. The stitches overlap and are not too long, so you do not have long threads on the surface which could catch and snag.

Using the darkest color and starting at the top of the shape, varying length stitches are added to the shape to fill it in. In the case of a curved object, the stitches are placed appropriate to the shape—this is often referred to as naturalistic shading (see the top left photo). In the case of a straight shape, the stitches can be made straight up and down the shape.

By having stitches that vary in length, when the next color is added, the area where both colors meet is blurred and the colors mix visually to create a smooth transition, rather than a lumpy look. Once the first color is added, bring the needle up through the fabric and through some of the embroidery stitches and take these new stitches down the shape and into the blank fabric. Again make sure that these stitches finish in a variety of different places. This technique continues until the shape is full (see diagrams center left).

This method of stitching is often referred to as thread painting, as it's a way of moving through colors and filling in a feature as you go—in a similar way to coloring in with pencils.

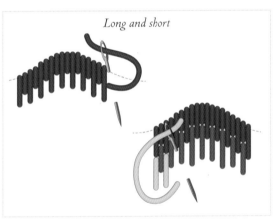

*Long and short*

## STAB STITCH

This is a tiny stitch often used to attach one fabric to another. Tiny stitches are used on the surface with bigger gaps on the back, so that layers of fabric are held together without the stitches being visible.

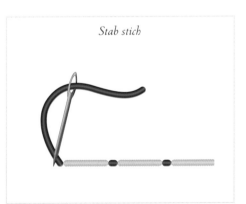

*Stab stich*

## SATIN STITCH

Working to shape outlines, satin stitch creates a solid fill of threads stitched directly next to each other so there are no visible gaps. The stitches should be as long on the front of the fabric as on the back, so you get an effect of the shape being padded.

It's a good idea to start in the middle of the shape and fill the edges to either side evenly, so that the correct angle of stitches is set in the middle and can be copied. Sometimes it's a good idea to add guide stitches to a shape to help you get the angle change set correctly before you start. Study the example on the left.

## PADDED SATIN STITCH

*Satin stitch*

*Padded satin stitch*

This is a layered filling-in stitch for a raised shape that is used to give the smooth, even appearance of satin. Numerous smooth, closely packed, long stitches are sewn side-by-side to evenly fill the shape, leaving no gaps. Start by outlining the shape with a split stitch edge. Begin in the middle of the shape, and working forward and outward, fill the shape. Angle the needle under the split stitch at the edges. The number of layers depends on the raised effect required.

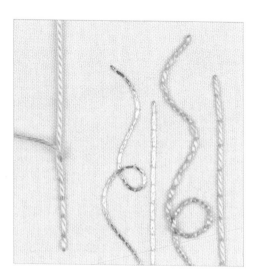

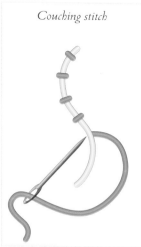

*Couching stitch*

## COUCHING

This is a good way of attaching a thread to fabric which would otherwise not be suitable to stitch with—for example, thick threads or metallic threads.

Couching technique can also be used to create very fine line details. Using a thin thread bring the needle up through the fabric and create small stitches over the thicker (couched) thread so it is held in place at regular intervals. In most cases the holding stitch is so small it's difficult to see.

# Projects

Better be...

Gryffindor

EXPECTO
PATRONUM

Our designs have been created using simple techniques that are suitable for the beginner and more experience stitcher alike. Full instructions are provided and each project has been given stitch levels of beginner ⚡, beginner/intermediate ⚡⚡, intermediate ⚡⚡⚡, and advanced ⚡⚡⚡⚡.

These levels will guide you through the different designs, while at the same time building your experience and knowledge as you work. Every design has photos to follow for each different aspect, including a reference to the stitch instructions so you know how each stitch is created. In many cases the same stitches are used, so you can hone your skills as you progress.

Once you have completed your projects you can display the hoop: simply use a ribbon to hang the hoop by the tightening screw. Alternatively sew a safety pin to the fabric on the back of the hoop so you can attach it to a nail to hang it up.

# GLASSES, SCARVES, AND SCAR

*"That ain't no ordinary cut on your forehead, Harry.*
*A mark like that only comes from being touched by a curse, and an evil curse at that."*

Harry Potter and the Sorcerer's Stone—*Hagrid*

## MATERIALS

**Fabric**—natural color, dress weight/quilt weight cotton

**Backing fabric**—unbleached natural cotton

**Suggested needles**—embroidery needle size 6 and 8, and chenille needle size 22

**Hoop**—6in (15.5cm) embroidery hoop for display. (You can use a 6in hoop to work on your embroidery but I prefer to have a little more room around the piece. My preference in this case would be a 8in (20.3cm) hoop in a stand so you can use both hands and not have to hold the hoop itself while you stitch.)

## STITCHES

Back stitch

Chain stitch

Couching stitch

Satin stitch

Tassels

## COLORS USED

1 x Black DMC 310

1 x Dark red DMC 815

1 x Flesh DMC 407

1 x Golden yellow DMC 3820

1 The frames of Harry's glasses are stitched with three strands of black. The solid fill is created with a back stitch leaving no visible space between the rows of stitches. Begin by adding a single row of back stitch around the edge of the frames and work inward. This very close method of back stitching creates a solid color for the glasses.

2 For the lightning bolt, use two strands of the flesh-tone thread and fill with satin stitch. Work the satin stitch across the shape (not along the shape) so the stitches are not too long. Once the satin stitch is complete, use a single thread of the same flesh color to add a couched edge round the shape—this will tidy all the edges and create a sharp angular shape.

### Note

The couched outline has the same color for both the couched thread and the stitching thread—flesh color.

3 Using chain stitch and two strands of golden yellow, work in each of the narrow bands of the scarves. All the lines of chain stitch are started on the inside edge of each scarf and worked outward. These rows of chain stitch slightly overshoot the edges of the scarves giving an uneven edge. This intentionally adds to the finished knitted look.

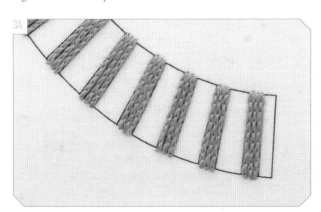

4 Once the golden yellow strips are complete, fill the gaps with dark red chain stitches. In this case, use three strands of DMC in the needle and slightly larger stitches. Each section in the example shown needed three complete rows, plus a part row. When using three strands of embroidery thread, work with the large gauge needle as this will make threading the needle much easier.

As the gaps to be filled with the dark red are wedge-shaped, add the first row on an edge, then add a part row next to that, completing the shape with two more rows. This part row will sort out the shape being wider on the outside—check the photos for reference.

5 Continue in the same way until all the chain stitch sections are filled for each of the four scarves.

6 When the scarf embroidery is finished, add the dark red tassels to the ends. These are stitched in place with a single strand of dark red thread.

Cut a 1.5 in (4 cm) length of stranded cotton in the same dark red color from the skein. This is folded in half and attached on the end of the scarf. In total seven small tassels are spaced evenly on the ends and attached at each end of the scarf—making fourteen on each scarf.

When the tassels are compete, trim them to the required length with sharp scissors.

GRYFFINDOR

# MISCHIEF MANAGED

*"I solemnly swear that I am up to no good."*

Harry Potter and the Prisoner of Azkaban—*George Weasley*

## MATERIALS

**Fabric**—parchment-colored dress weight/quilt weight cotton

**Backing fabric**—unbleached natural cotton

**Suggested needles**—embroidery needle size 6 and 8, and chenille needle size 22

**Hoop**—6in (15.5cm) embroidery hoop for display. (You can use a 6in hoop to work on your embroidery but I prefer to have a little more room around the piece. My preference in this case would be a 8in (20.3cm) hoop in a stand so you can use both hands and not have to hold the hoop itself while you stitch.)

## STITCHES

Back stitch

Chain stitch

Couching stitch

Long-short stitch

Satin stitch

## COLORS USED

1 x Dark red DMC 815

1 x Purple DMC 29

1 With two strands of dark red and the long and short technique, add vertical stitches inside the diamond shape in the middle of the design. This dense stitching will create a solid fill of color.

### Note

If you cannot buy a suitable fabric to look like parchment you can dye your own. In this case I used a cream-colored fabric and dyed it in a strong solution of English breakfast tea.

### Fabric dyeing

Use two teabags in a cup of hot/warm water. Scrunch up your fabric into a ball and place it into the cup, leave for up to a minute, and then remove and rinse. You will find the fabric has taken on an aged look with a greater intensity of color along the creases.

When dry this will look aged and more like the parchment map. Some experimentation might be needed to get the right color and look you're after.

2 When the diamond is completely filled, the edge of this shape can be finished off with a couching stitch to make the sides crisp and straight. The couching stitch in this case was done with two strands of the same dark red shade, plus a single strand of the same shade to hold the thread in place.

Thread two strands of purple in the needle, create a chain stitch around the outside edge of the red diamond. Check out the design for the position of this line.

3 Using purple thread, surface couch a line around the outside of the ribbon sections which contain the text "Mischief Managed." Three strands of threads are used on the surface of the embroidery, with a single strand of purple used to keep the surface thread in position.

### Tip

*When working chain stitch lines that come up to sharp points, stitch all the lines as separate features. This will preserve the sharp edges and prevent the points becoming rounded and untidy.*

4 With two threads of purple in the needle, use a back stitch to outline the design.

Continue using a further two threads of purple in the needle, use back stitch to fill in the lettering. See the photo for guidance.

5 Using satin stitch and two strands of purple thread in the needle, fill in the shapes of the footprints. In each case start stitching in the middle of the shoe and work out to the sides. For each footprint, note how the angle of the satin stitch has been slightly adjusted to follow the direction of the footprint itself.

# DOBBY IS A FREE ELF

*"You shall not harm Harry Potter!"*

Harry Potter and the Chamber of Secrets—*Dobby*

## MATERIALS

**Fabric**—white cotton

**Backing fabric**—unbleached natural cotton

**Suggested needles** —embroidery needle size 6 and 8, and chenille needle size 22

**Hoop**—6in (15.5cm) embroidery hoop for display. (You can use a 6in hoop to work on your embroidery but I prefer to have a little more room around the piece. My preference in this case would be a 8in (20.3cm) hoop in a stand so you can use both hands and not have to hold the hoop itself while you stitch.)

## STITCHES

Back stitch

Chain stitch

French knots

Running stitch

Satin stitch

Split stitch

Straight stitch

## COLORS USED

x 1 Black DMC 310

x 1 Brown/sage DMC 640

x 1 Dark red DMC 815

x 1 Golden yellow DMC 3820

x 1 Lime green DMC 165

x 1 Metallic silver DMC E168

1 Using two strands of a metallic silver thread, stitch the dashed lines with a running stitch that covers the printed dashes. Once the running stitch is complete, use the same metallic thread to add small crossed stitches across the background, plus some straight stitches on the sock and the finger-click circles around Dobby's hand.

### Tip

*For the metallic thread use a large-eyed needle with a sharp point. This makes a larger hole in the fabric that protects the thread from being damaged and makes stitching easier.*

2 Using two strands of lime green, add satin stitch to the circles inside Dobby's eyes.

With the same thread, add French knots to the dots on the background behind Dobby.

## Tip

*French knots can be made with a single wrap of thread on the needle (or more). Using two wraps of thread to create the knot just makes it bigger.*

3 With two strands of brown/sage, use split stitch to cover the lines of Dobby's clothes.

4 Working with back stitch, outline Dobby with a single strand of black thread. Do the same to the outline of the sock.

Using the same thread, add these extra details:

- French knots to the eyes—in this case just a single wrap of thread will create a big enough knot. (2A)
- Single decorative stitches to either side of the single metallic lines on the finger click. (4B)
- Decorative lines to the sock—look at the photo for exact details. (4C)
- Back stitch to cover lines of hair. (7A)

**5** Cover the border lines around the design using chain stitch and two strands of dark red thread. Check out the photos for the exact placements.

**7** Using two strands of dark red thread, use split stitch to embroider the letters.

**6** The remaining border lines are also stitched with chain stitch, but this time use golden yellow thread. Again see the photo for reference.

**8** With two strands of dark red thread sew straight and split stitches to add color to the letters.

# EXPECTO PATRONUM

*" . . . this is very advanced magic, well beyond the Ordinary Wizarding Level."*

Harry Potter and the Prizoner of Azkaban—*Professor Lupin*

## MATERIALS

**Fabric**—light gray/parchment color, dress weight/quilt weight cotton

**Backing fabric**—unbleached natural cotton

**Suggested needles** —embroidery needle size 6 and 8, and chenille needle size 22

**Hoop**—6in (15.5cm) embroidery hoop for display. (You can use a 6in hoop to work on your embroidery but I prefer to have a little more room around the piece. My preference in this case would be a 8in (20.3cm) hoop in a stand so you can use both hands and not have to hold the hoop itself while you stitch.)

## STITCHES

Back stitch

Couched stitch

French knot

Stem stitch

Straight stitch

## COLORS USED

1 x Black DMC 310

1 x Mid gray DMC 317

1 x Metallic diamant thread DMC D168

1 x Mid blue DMC 334

1 x reel Light gray general purpose machine thread (Gutermann Sew All. Col:8)

## Note

Color key showing which technique is used for each line:

| Color | Thread | Stitch |
|---|---|---|
| Green | Black DMC 310 | back stitch |
| Dark blue | Mid gray DMC 317 | stem stitch |
| Turquoise | Mid gray DMC 317 | back stitch |
| Yellow | Mid blue DMC 334 | back stitch |
| Orange | Metallic silver diamant D168 | couched thread |
| Black circles | Metallic silver diamant D168 | French knots |
| Pink lines | Metallic silver diamant D168 | decorative straight stitches |

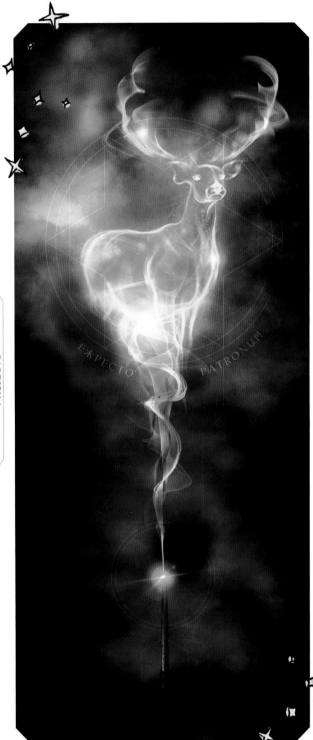

1 Using two strands of the mid-blue thread, fill the all the letters using back stitch.

2 With a single strand of black thread, add a back stitch over the lines on the design shown in the photo. (The color key on the previous page will help you with the placement of the lines.)

### Tip
*The stitches need to be kept small and neat as many of the lines follow curves.*

3 Take two strands of mid gray, and add a stem stitch over the lines on the design shown in the picture. (Use the color key on page 49 as reference.)

(Use the color key on page 49 as reference.)

design shown in the picture.

### Tip

*When working lines which come up to sharp points, stitch both lines as separate features, this will preserve the sharp edges and prevent the points becoming rounded and untidy.*

4 Using two strands of mid gray, add back stitch over the lines of the eyeball, eyelid, and bottom of the nose—these lines are too short to use stem stitch. (Use the color key as reference.)

4A

5 With a single strand of mid-blue thread, add back stitch over the lines on the design indicated in the photo. (Use the color key as reference.)

5A

## Note

Color key showing which technique is used for each line:

| Color | Thread | Stitch |
|---|---|---|
| Green | Black DMC 310 | back stitch |
| Dark blue | Mid gray DMC 317 | stem stitch |
| Turquoise | Mid gray DMC 317 | back stitch |
| Yellow | Mid blue DMC 334 | back stitch |

6  Add couched lines over the remaining design lines using two strands of silver metallic thread as the surface thread, plus a single strand of light gray machine thread as the sewing thread.

### Tip
*Your couching stitches should be as small as possible so they are not seen on the surface of the embroidery*

7  Add French knots to the middle of the stags eye using two strands of silver metallic thread. (Use the color key as a reference.)

8  Using a needle threaded with a single strand of silver metallic thread, stitch over the stars in the background.

### Note
Color key showing which technique is used for each line:

| Color | Thread | Stitch |
| --- | --- | --- |
| Orange | Metallic silver diamant D168 | couched thread |
| Black circles | Metallic silver diamant D168 | French knots |
| Pink lines | Metallic silver diamant D168 | decorative straight stitches |

# IT'S *LEVIOSA*, NOT *LEVIOSA*

*"Besides, you're saying it wrong. It's LeviOsa, not LeviosA."*

Harry Potter and the Sorcerer's Stone—*Hermione Granger*

## MATERIALS

**Fabric**—light blue dress weight/quilt weight cotton

**Backing fabric**—unbleached natural cotton

**Suggested needles**—embroidery needle size 6 and 8, and chenille needle size 22

**Hoop**—6in (15.5cm) embroidery hoop for display. (You can use a 6in hoop to work on your embroidery but I prefer to have a little more room around the piece. My preference in this case would be a 8in (20.3cm) hoop in a stand so you can use both hands and not have to hold the hoop itself while you stitch.)

## STITCHES

Back stitch

Chain stitch

Couching stitch

Satin stitch

Stem stitch

## COLORS USED

1 x Beige DMC 543

1 x Brown DMC 801

1 x Dark blue DMC 796

1 x Dark brown DMC 938

1 x Light brown DMC 3863

1 x Mid blue DMC 809

1 Using two strands of dark blue add a back stitch solid fill to the letters—excluding the large "O" and the "A."

2 With two strands of mid blue, work satin stitch over the capital "O" and the capital "A." To add further definition to the letters, add a couched outline. The couched outline is stitched using two strands for the surface thread, and a single stand as the stitching thread all in the same shade as the mid blue of the satin stitch.

3 Using two strands of beige, add stem stitch through the central quill of the feather. These lines of stem stitch are used to completely fill this middle shape.

PROJECTS

4 Starting at the tip of the feather, use two strands of beige to add a couched edge to the outline of the first feather blade (using two strands as the surface thread, and a single strand as the stitching thread). This will create a really nice, sharply defined edge. As you work down the shape, change the outer feather blade color to the appropriate shade.

Once the feather shapes are outlined they are filled with rows of chain stitch. Use two strands in the needle. Start on the outside edge of the shape and work inwards. I suggest you vary the colors you use for the chain stitch, so that overall the feather gets darker towards the base. Try to make each of the shapes look slightly different, so that they stand out against each other.

As the chain stitch is worked with two threads in the needle, you can mix the colors to create a subtle color change.

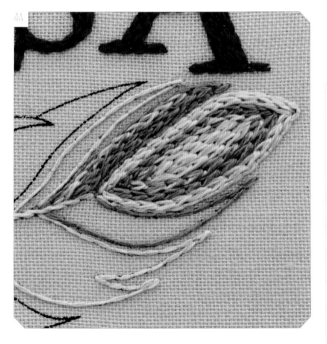

*Tip*

*When working chain stitch lines which come up to sharp points, stitch all lines as separate features, this will preserve the sharpness and prevent the points becoming rounded and untidy.*

This is one possible color combination:
2 x DMC 543, 1 x DMC 543, 1 x DMC 3863, 2 x DMC 3863, 1 x DMC 3863, 1 x DMC 801, 2 x DMC 801, 1 x DMC 801, 1 x DMC 938, 2 x DMC 938

Color Key

| | |
|---|---|
| ⬛ | Reference to DMC 801 |
| | Reference to DMC 543, DMC 3863, and DMC 801 |
| | Reference to DMC 938 |
| | Reference to DMC 938 and DMC 801 |
| | Reference to DMC 543 |
| | Reference to DMC 543 and DMC 3863 |
| | Reference to DMC 3863 |

# HOGWARTS CASTLE

⚡⚡⚡

*"Help will always be given at Hogwarts, Harry, to those who ask for it."*

Harry Potter and the Deathly Hallows, Part 2—*Albus Dumbledore*

## MATERIALS

**Fabric** – white cotton

**Backing fabric**—unbleached natural cotton

**Suggested needles** —embroidery needle size 6 and 8, and chenille needle size 22

**Hoop**—6in (15.5cm) embroidery hoop for display. (You can use a 6in hoop to work on your embroidery but I prefer to have a little more room around the piece. My preference in this case would be a 8in (20.3cm) hoop in a stand so you can use both hands and not have to hold the hoop itself while you stitch.)

## STITCHES

Back stitch

Couching

Satin stitch

## COLORS USED

1 x Glow in the dark DMC 940
or 1 x Bright white DMC 01
1 x Black DMC 310
1 x Light gray DMC 04
1 x Mid gray DMC 03

1 With two strands of the luminous (glow in the dark) or bright white thread, sew satin stitch into each of the window shapes.

2 Use a single strand of black to add a fine surface couching over the long straight lines of the roof tops and tower walls. The single strand of embroidery thread is held in place with a single strand of the same color as the holding stitches.

For shorter lines on the building, a single black stitch can be used over the design lines.

3 Once all the school building is completely covered in black stitches —this will take some time and patience—you can move onto the cliffs beneath.

Two shades of thread are needed to add a little shading to the cliffs. Thread your needle with a single strand each of light gray and mid gray and use it to add back stitches over the lines of the cliffs.

## Note

If you want to add color to the finished school scene you can use a very weak wash of blue watercolor paint to add sky to the background and gray shading to the cliffs. BUT always add color slowly as you can add more if (when completely dry) the effect is not as strong as you want. Remember, colors always look darker when wet.

# DARK MARK

*"The terror it inspired . . . you have no idea, you're too young.
Just picture coming home and finding the Dark Mark hovering over your house . . . "*

Harry Potter and the Goblet of Fire—*Arthur Weasley*

## MATERIALS

**Fabric**—mid gray cotton

**Backing fabric**—unbleached natural
cotton

**Suggested needles** —embroidery
needle size 6 and 8, and chenille
needle size 22

**Hoop**—6in (15.5cm) embroidery
hoop for display. (You can use
a 6in hoop to work on your
embroidery but I prefer to have a
little more room around the piece.
My preference in this case would
be a 8in (20.3cm) hoop in a stand
so you can use both hands and not
have to hold the hoop itself while
you stitch.)

## STITCHES

Back stitch

Couching stitch

Padded Satin stitch

Running stitch

Satin stitch

Straight stitch

## COLORS USED

1 x Black DMC 310

1 x Glow in the dark DMC E940

1 x Light gray polyester machine
thread

1 x Metallic silver DMC E168

1 x Mid gray DMC 317

1 x Neon green DMC E990

1 x Orange DMC 976

1 Using two strands of the glow in the dark thread, add padded satin
stitch to the two eye socket areas and the nose cavity on the skull. With a
further two strands of glow in the dark thread, add satin stitch to the teeth
to finish the skull.

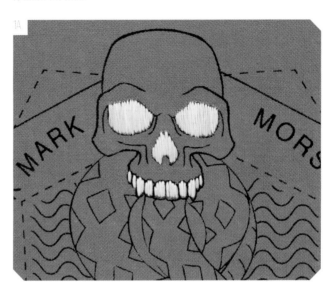

2 Using two strands of mid gray, satin stitch the diamond shapes on the
body of the snake.

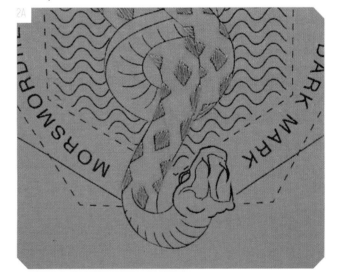

3 The lines of dashes are stitched using two strands of neon green. These lines are worked with a running stitch matching the dashed lines on the design.

4 Use satin stitch and two strands of orange to create the eye of the snake.

With one strand of the glow in the dark thread, add some straight stitches into the fangs of the snake.

5 Use two strands of the silver metallic thread to sew large stitches around the solid hexagon shape. Break these long stitches up with small black diamonds in the corners. Use a single strand of mid gray as the holding stitch to couch this metallic thread down securely to the fabric. By using this mid gray, the stitches are very subtle and the silver becomes the dominant color—adding to the spookiness.

## Tip

*Thin, strong polyester thread is most effective for holding down metallic threads.*

6 The inner hexagon has a wave pattern background. This wave pattern is stitched using the surface couching method with a single strand of the metallic silver thread. The metallic thread is held in position using a pale gray polyester machine thread. In this case the stitches should be small, with only a tiny gap between the stitches.

7 Lines on the underside belly of the snake are stitched with a double running stitch and in this case a single strand of neon green. Check out the photos for exact references.

8 With two strands of black thread, add satin stitch over the diamond shapes at the points of the silver hexagon.

With two strands of black thread, add back stitch around the outline of both the skull and the snake.

Using two strands of black thread, add back stitch over all the lettering. Keep checking against the photos to get it right.

### Tip
*Glow in the dark thread is activated by natural or artificial light. If you use a black light, which you can buy online, it will glow brighter and longer.*

# HOGWARTS CREST

*"Never Tickle a Sleeping Dragon"*

Hogwarts school motto

## MATERIALS

**Fabric**—white cotton

**Backing fabric**—unbleached natural cotton

**Suggested needles**—embroidery needle size 6 and 8, and chenille needle size 22

**Hoop**—6in (15.5cm) embroidery hoop for display. (You can use a 6in hoop to work on your embroidery but I prefer to have a little more room around the piece. My preference in this case would be a 8in (20.3cm) hoop in a stand so you can use both hands and not have to hold the hoop itself while you stitch.)

## STITCHES

Back stitch

Couching stitch

Satin stitch

Stem stitch

Straight stitch

## COLORS USED

1 x Black DMC 310

1 x Blue DMC 796

1 x Dark gray DMC 317

1 x Dark red DMC 815

1 x Golden yellow DMC 3820

1 x Green DMC 699

1 x Light gray DMC 03

1 x Metallic silver DMC E168

1 x Mid gray DMC 04

1 x Yellow DMC 444

1 x White DMC B5200

1 For the black text of the crest, use two strands of black-stranded cotton. Use a back stitch inside the shapes to fill in the letters. To finish off and make them look really crisp, use a single strand of black thread to create a fine back stitch round the edges to fill in any white gaps that may have been left.

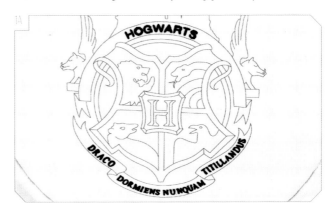

2 Crest backgrounds: Embroider diagonal stitches using two strands of the relevant color for each house in each of the four quarters of the crest to fill in the background.

Gryffindor lion—dark red

Slytherin snake—green

Ravenclaw raven—blue

Hufflepuff badger—yellow

### Tip
*Start the diagonal lines in the middle of the shape and set the angle you want to follow. This first stitch can be used to help line up others either side.*

3 At the top of the design there is a silhouette of Hogwarts Castle, outline this shape using two strands of dark gray with a back stitch.

On either side of the crest there is a winged hog mystical beast. Outline these winged creatures in stem stitch using two strands in the needle of the same dark gray. The blocks these beasts stand on are stitched with straight stitches and two strands of dark gray.

4 Thread a single strand of dark gray and embroider back stitch across the middle section of the crest around each of the animal characters of the four houses.

5 Use a single strand of black thread and back stitch to go around the central black capital "H." The darker lines in the middle of the letter are created using chain stitch with a single strand of the same black thread, to make it really stand out.

6 Using two strands of silver metallic thread, stitch two circular inner lines behind the crest. Hold this in position with a surface couching stitch. Here the silver metallic thread is held in position using a single strand of white thread.

## Tip
*Metallic threads can be difficult to use as they break easily and can knot going through fabric. Use a technique like couching to hold them on the surface of the fabric. Alternatively, use larger needles that create bigger holes in the fabric and therefore make the thread easier to use.*

7 The banners at the top and bottom of the crest both need outlining using surface couched threads. Use five strands of the light gray thread held on the surface and a single strand as the couching stitch to hold these threads in position. Make sure the stitches are held tight on the ends of the lines to maintain nice sharp points at the ends of the ribbons.

8 In the small folded sections of the text ribbons there are four small triangles. On each of these use satin stitch with two strands of mid gray to create the underside of the ribbon and the appearance of shadows.

9 Use two threads of golden yellow in the needle to stitch the crest border with satin stitch.

Once the border is covered in satin stitch, the edges need to be neatened off with a couched thread in the same color as the satin stitch (golden yellow). Use three strands held on the surface along the edge, plus a single strand of the same color as the holding stitch.

### Tip

*To help keep your satin stitch at the correct angle you can add pencil lines inside the border. These will be hidden with the stitching, but this will help keep you on track.*

# SORTING HAT

⚡⚡⚡⚡

*". . . but where to put you . . ."*

Harry Potter and the Sorcerer's Stone—*The Sorting Hat*

## MATERIALS

**Fabric**—cream dress weight/quilt weight cotton

**Backing fabric**—unbleached natural cotton

**Suggested needles**—embroidery needle size 6 and 8, and chenille needle size 22

**Hoop**—6in (15.5cm) embroidery hoop for display. (You can use a 6in hoop to work on your embroidery but I prefer to have a little more room around the piece. My preference in this case would be a 8in (20.3cm) hoop in a stand so you can use both hands and not have to hold the hoop itself while you stitch.)

## STITCHES

Back stitch

Chain stitch

Couching stitch

French knot

Long and short stitches

Split stitch

## COLORS USED

1 x Black DMC 310

1 x Dark brown DMC 801

1 x Dark red DMC 815

1 x Dark orange DMC 919

1 x Darkest brown DMC 938

1 x Light brown DMC 434

1 x Mid brown DMC 433

1 x Very dark brown DMC 898

1 Using two strands of dark orange, sew a chain stitch around the circular border. You may need to do three lines of this depending on the tension of your stitches.

2 When the chain stitch in the border is complete, use three strands of black thread as a couched thread around the inside and outside edge of the border. Use a single strand of the same black color as the stitching thread to hold the couched thread in place. This completes the two-color border ring.

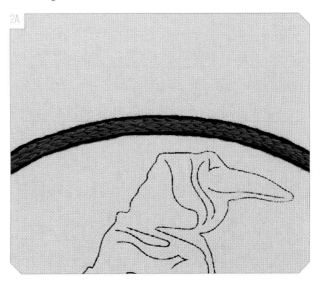

3 Use two strands of black thread to embroider split stitches over the words "Better be" on the design. For the three dots add a French knot over the top of each one using the same black thread.

3A

4 With three strands of dark red, add a back stitch to fill each of the letters of the text "Gryffindor."

4A

5 Using two strands of the very dark brown (DMC 898), add long and short stitches running directly down the fabric over the eyes and mouth of the hat. With two strands of lightest brown (DMC434) add long and short stitches running down the fabric for the patch area.

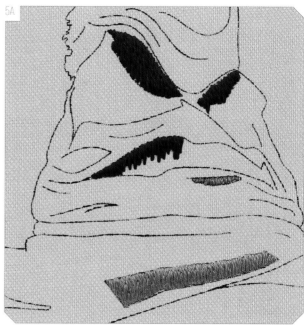
5A

6 Using two stands of dark brown (DMC 801), add long and short stitches around the areas of the eyes, the mouth, the shadow of the hat fold at the top, and the underside of the hat's brim. See the color key at the top of the next page for the exact references.

6A

7 Using two strands of the middle tone of brown (DMC 433), add long and short stitches in the areas shown by the color key.

8 Using two strands of the darkest tone of brown (DMC 938), add long and short stitches in the remaining areas of the hat.

### Color Key

| | | | |
|---|---|---|---|
| ⬛ | Reference to DMC 898 | ⬜ | Reference to DMC 434 |
| 🟫 | Reference to DMC 433 | 🟫 | Reference to DMC 801 |
| ⬜ | Reference to DMC 938 | | |

# PLATFORM 9¾

⚡⚡⚡⚡

*"But, Hagrid, there must be a mistake! This says Platform 9¾.
There's no such thing! Is there?"*

Harry Potter and the Sorcerer's Stone—*Harry Potter*

## MATERIALS

**Fabric**—white dress weight/quilt weight cotton and dark red dress weight/quilt weight cotton

**Backing fabric**—unbleached natural cotton

**Suggested needles**—embroidery needle size 6 and 8, and chenille needle size 22

**Hoop**—6in (15.5cm) embroidery hoop for display. (You can use a 6in hoop to work on your embroidery but I prefer to have a little more room around the piece. My preference in this case would be a 8in (20.3cm) hoop in a stand so you can use both hands and not have to hold the hoop itself while you stitch.)

## STITCHES

Chain stitch

Couching stitches

Long and short stitches

Satin stitch

Stab stitches

Straight stitch

## COLORS USED

2 x Black DMC 310

1 x Golden yellow DMC 3820

1 x reel Black general purpose machine thread (Gutermann Sew All Col: 1)

1 This project involves stitching on two different background color fabrics, and then using them stitched together so the finished embroidery matches the original logo as closely as possible.

First set up the embroidery hoop with the white fabric and the backing fabric. This is so the numbers can be embroidered and the background red fabric won't show through when it is attached behind later.

2 Using two strands of black thread, add long and short stitches over the numbers to create a solid fill of color. When this is complete, add a couched line of black around all the numbers to make the edges as neat as possible. For the couching use two stands of black thread on the surface and a single strand in the needle to hold this thread in place.

As this design is a recognized trademark there are also the ™ letters to embroider. These are worked with a straight stitch and a single strand of black thread in the needle.

3 Once the embroidery on the white fabric is complete, carefully cut out the finished circle. Cut it out just inside the outer circle, thus ensuring it fits inside of the dark red backing fabric.

2A

3A

4 Set up the dark-red fabric, white circle, and backing fabric onto your ring frame. Don't make them too taut. You are adding a loose fabric over the top of the background fabric—so all the fabrics need to be at a similar tension.

With a black general-purpose sewing thread, stitch around the outside of the white circle of embroidery holding it in the correct place with stab stitches. These stab stitches should be no more than 0.25 inches apart and are worked by bringing the needle up through the dark-red fabric, then up through the white fabric, all along the line of the outer circle. Once you have worked round the circle, the fabrics should be firmly attached together. Now we can continue with the stitching to cover the join.

### Note
Do not make your stab stitches/holding stitches any longer than the inner circle or they will show when the embroidery is finished.

5 Now that the white fabric is stitched firmly in place, the red background fabric can be pulled tight to continue stitching.

Using two strands of black thread, add satin stitch all around the outside of the white fabric and the border of the "PLATFORM" text.

6 Work satin stitch around the circle so that it follows the flow of the shape. The border for the text is worked in satin stitch and follows the curve of the circle along the top, and on a diagonal for the short sides.

Again to finish this feature off, a couched line is added on all sides. Use four strands of black thread for the surface thread and a single strand of the same color for the sewing stitch.

For the outer circle border use a single thread of golden yellow and chain stitch, followed by a couched edge.

Using two strands of golden yellow thread, add two rows of chain stitch just inside the ring to make a solid fill pattern.

Once this is complete, the ring is finished off on both edges with a couched detail. For this couching use three strands of golden yellow thread on the surface, and a single strand as the stitching thread.

*Tip*

*You will find it easier working from above to below—from the white fabric into the red fabric. Pushing the needle down into many layers of fabric is much easier than working up.*

7 Fill the letters of "PLATFORM" with satin stitch. For this use two strands of golden yellow thread to embroider satin stitch inside the letter shapes. Once these letters are filled, the edges can again be tidied up with a couched edge. In this case, only a single strand of thread in golden yellow is used on the surface with a single strand used as the holding stitch. This gives the lettering a nice crisp, official-looking, edge.

# ABOUT THE AUTHOR

## DEBORAH WILDING

Originally from Carlisle in Cumbria, and now
based in North Somerset in England's West
Country, Deborah Wilding specializes in hand
embroidery, using traditional methods to
produce work of exceptionally high quality.
Her studio space is located in the seafront area
of North Somerset, looking out over the Bristol
Channel towards Wales. A setting she finds truly
inspirational.

Deborah is highly trained in historically accurate
techniques, including goldwork, silk shading,
whitework, blackwork, and crewelwork among
many other needlework techniques. As well as
working on freelance embroidery projects, she
also teaches embroidery skills on behalf of the
Royal School of Needlework (RSN) in private
companies.

After completing the RSN's "Future Tutor"
course (the world's leading educational
establishment for the teaching of hand
embroidery to a professional level) and
graduating with distinction in 2015, Deborah
has been employed by the RSN to teach on both
their Certificate and Diploma Programme and
their extensive Day Class Programme, both in the
UK and abroad.

In her freelance capacity, she works from her
seaside studio on day class designs, restoration
projects, and private commissions, as well as
teaching private lessons.

### Dedication
I would like to thank my husband
Chris for his continued support and
encouragement. Also, my children Joe
and Livvy, whose love and knowledge of
the Harry Potter stories has inspired me
when stitching these designs.